Dreams Like Mine

Photographs and Poems

DAVID JENNINGS

RESOURCE *Publications* • Eugene, Oregon

DREAMS LIKE MINE
Photographs and Poems

Resource Publications
An Imprint of Wipf and Stock Publishers
199 W. 8th Ave., Suite 3
Eugene, OR 97401

www.wipfandstock.com

PAPERBACK ISBN: 979-8-3852-5581-8
HARDCOVER ISBN: 979-8-3852-5582-5
EBOOK ISBN: 979-8-3852-5583-2

Dreams Like Mine

Thank you, Kristin and Reagan
I love you

For my brother, Robert
(September 3–5, 1968)

Acknowledgements

My thanks to J Hall and the Okie Bookcast for previously publishing the poems on pages 35, 36, 43, and 70 in his podcast, Behind the Rain: Oklahoma Poetry Anthology.

My thanks to the publishers of The Lyric for previously publishing the poems on pages 6, 9, 11, and 47.

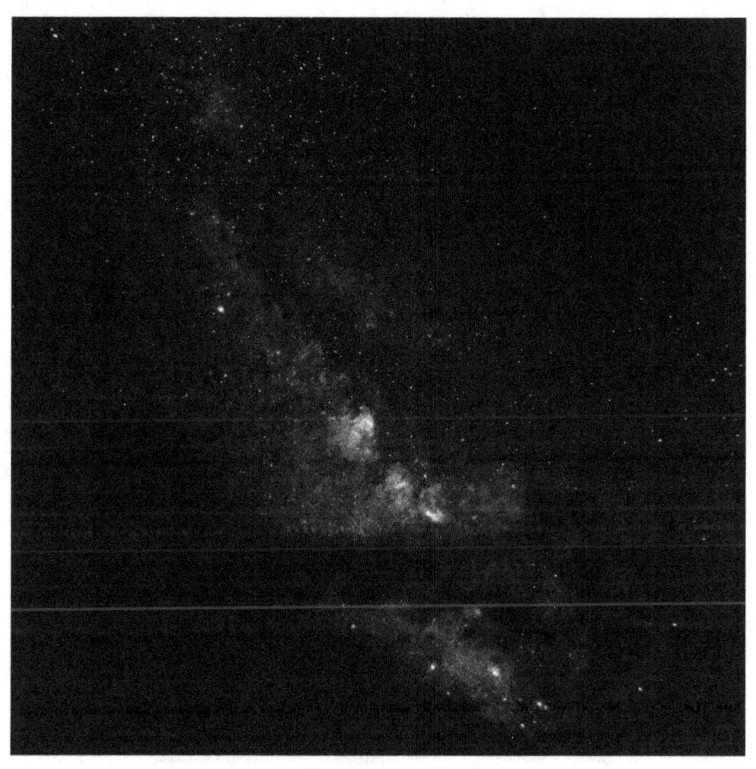

Once there was no day or night,
black without a whit of white—
not one glint to offer sight.
Then God said, *Let there be light.*
Look up! The edge of heaven's height
shimmers now, if ever slight.

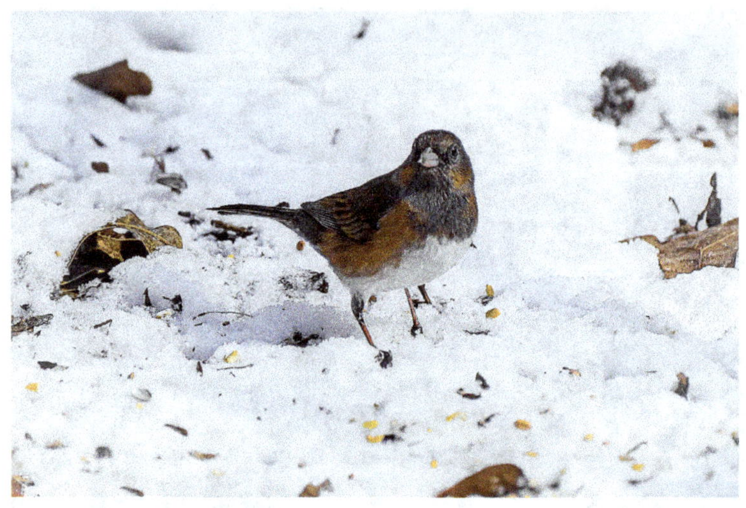

I wish I could tell you take cover, stay warm!
Get ready, sweet bird, for this incoming storm.
Eat all of the seed you can possibly eat
for fire in your belly to shiver for heat.
Start early—eat often, before it moves in.
I hope through the fall you have padded your skin.
I wish I could tell you to tell all your friends
go find a deep hollow away from the winds.
Perhaps that wild undergrowth crowding the wall
would be a safe place to escape from a squall.
Get back there as far as the thicket permits
and huddle together until the storm quits.

I wish I could warn you and help you prepare—
or turn and pretend that I don't even care.

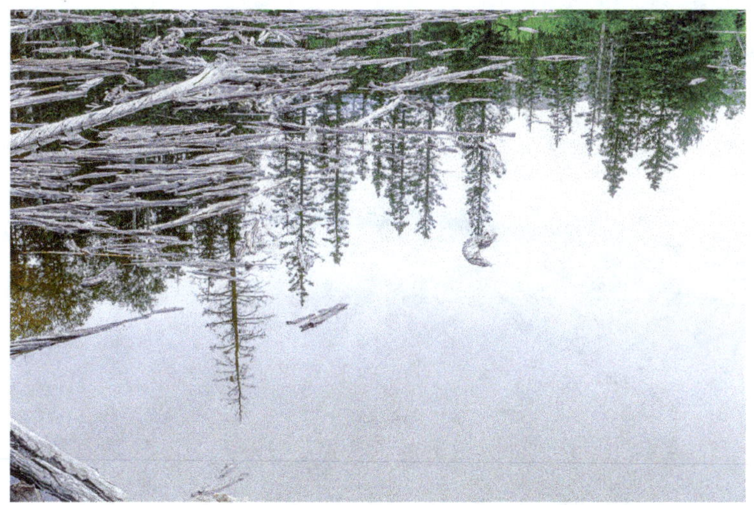

Sometimes an image
flipped, reflected
goes at first as
undetected.
But once seen and
flipped, corrected
ends up stunningly
perfected.

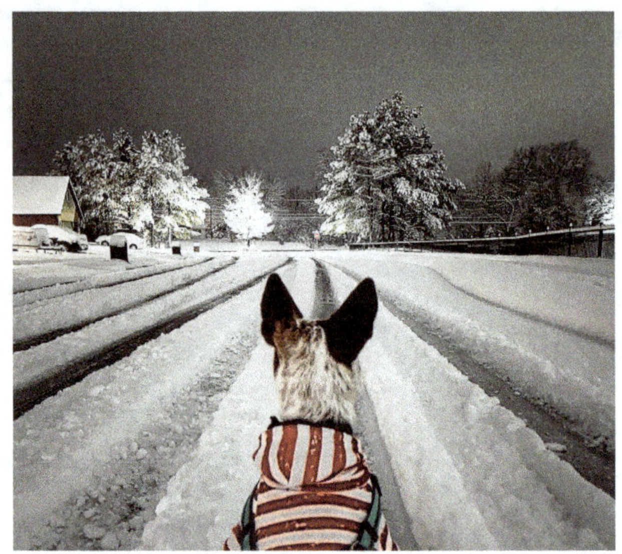

Imagine my shock
when I went out to walk
and the whole place was covered in white!
I sat down to gawk
in butt-freezing chalk
and to study the staggering sight.
Then I slid down the block
(a leashed laughingstock)
with my dad slipping left, slipping right!

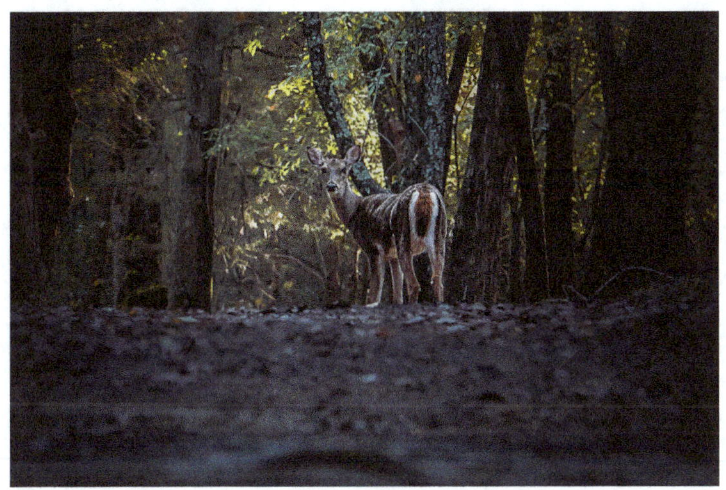

Be careful when men walk the wood.
Best find a place to hide
until you know they're gone for good,
and then assume you're spied
from some tall perch or hidden fort
by eyes behind a gun.
When the wood echoes report
I pray you're not the one.

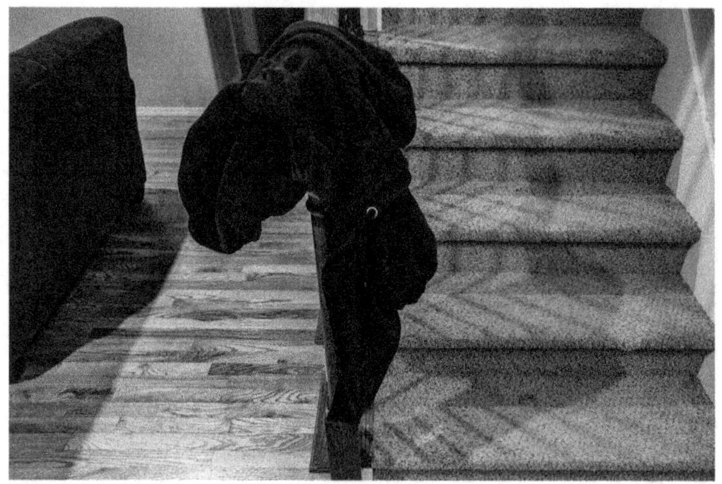

Leave the sweatshirt on the stair.
The day will come when she will say
Goodbye. And wave. And drive away.
And then that sweatshirt won't be there.
Nor will those shoes that strew the hall—
the pens and books that spread across
the countertop, the dental floss
left in the sink, and hair! They all
will go away when she is gone.
And then—so what? The house is neat.
The floors lack flaws from little feet.
The mirrors shine. And on. And on.
Leave the sweatshirt on the stair—
remind me of this answered prayer.

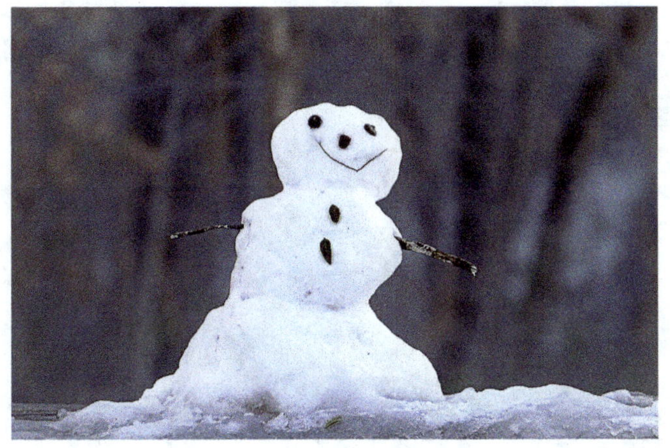

My snow you scooped
and piled and packed.
My three parts
you shaped and stacked.
Two twigs like arms
(they're not exact).
Two eyes, a nose
from acorns hacked.
Only one thing
more I lacked:
a mouth to show
a smile or frown.
For you, I'll grin
while melting down.

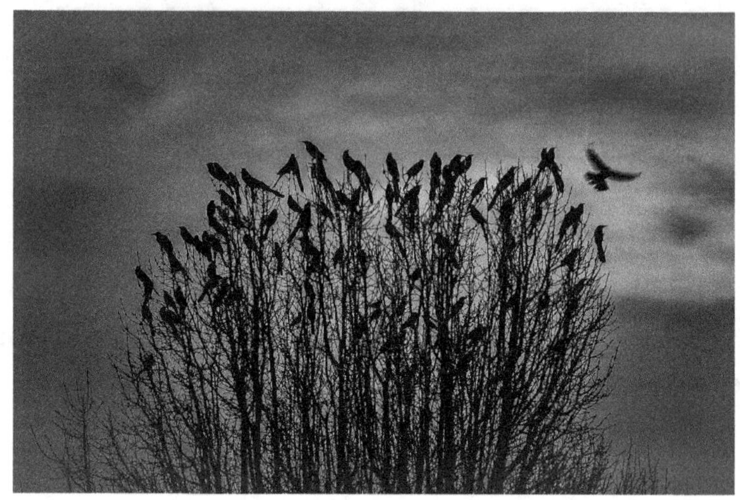

At dusk we fill the empty bough
(as many as the limbs allow)
and jabber on about our day.
A man moans with his bothered brow,
I've got to get some sleep somehow!
and rubs his eyes and walks away.

At dawn we rouse the empty bough
(as many as the limbs allow)
and prattle on about our night.
A man moans with his bothered brow,
I've had no sleep sixteen nights now!
and stomps and we all flinch in fright.

At dusk we plan to reconvene
and try to make it seventeen.

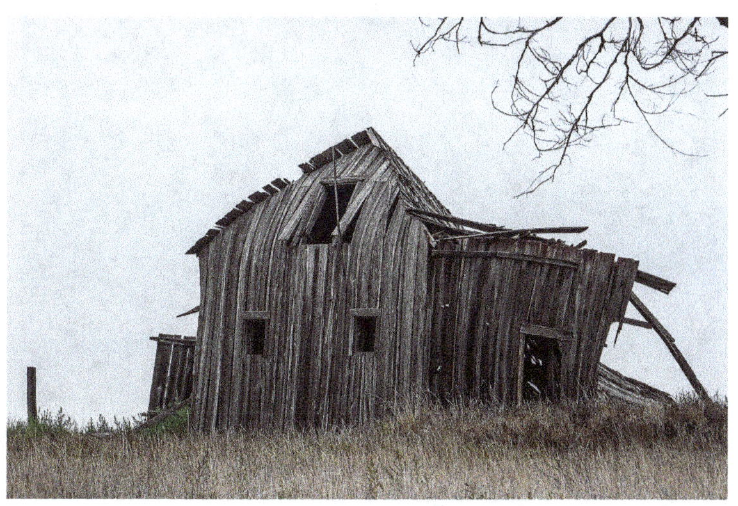

I can no longer stand up straight.
In fact, the toll of time and weight
of snow and ice and soak of rain
and blow of wind across the plain
have caused my frame to list and shift
as each bent board begins to lift
away from nails that once held true.
Now my roof has fallen through.

Next will come the crumpling sound
of me collapsing to the ground.

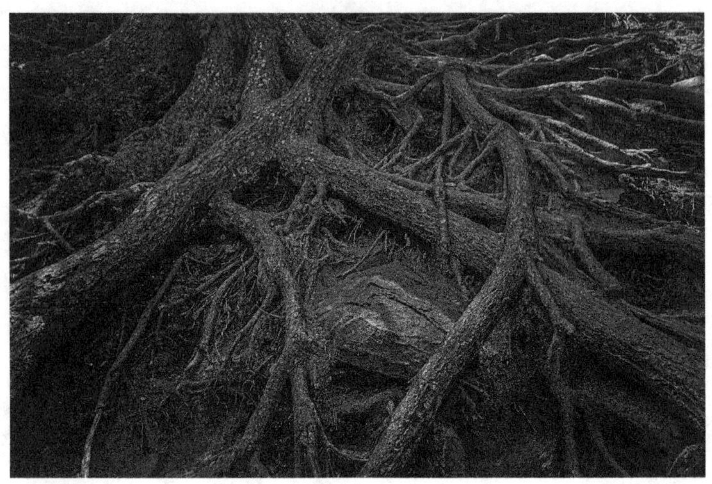

Grow my faith
like thirsting roots
that grip
to rock and ground.
Stand me steady
—tethered, taut—
to keep
from being downed.
Draw me anchored
close to You
with sinker roots
delved deep
that stay me sturdy
even where
the soil is
loose and steep.

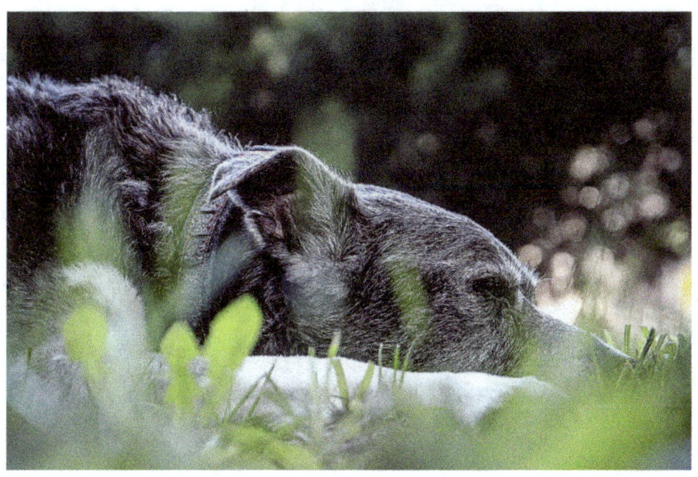

One last time—my paws in dirt.
My belly resting on the grass.
My nose, from time to time alert,
to sniff some odor drifting past.
One last time—my ears to hear
a bird's tree-hidden, joyful call.
My eyes (although with age unclear)
to squint and watch the shadows fall.
One last time for me to know
this house, this yard, this world I've had.
One last time—before we go—
to spend a morning with my dad.

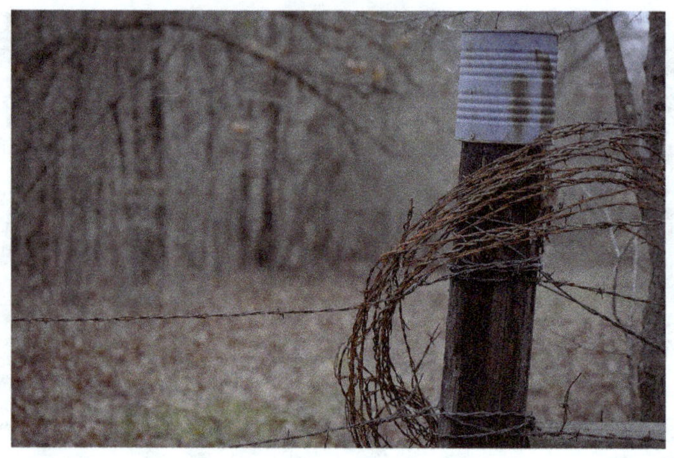

Long ago
my posts were set
and barbed wire drawn
as if to let
the neighbor know
That's all you get!
My land starts here,
lest you forget—
or perhaps
to curb the threat
from horse or cow
or wandering pet.
The wire rusts now
with barbed regret:
for years two men
shared soil and yet
we kept our own
and never met.

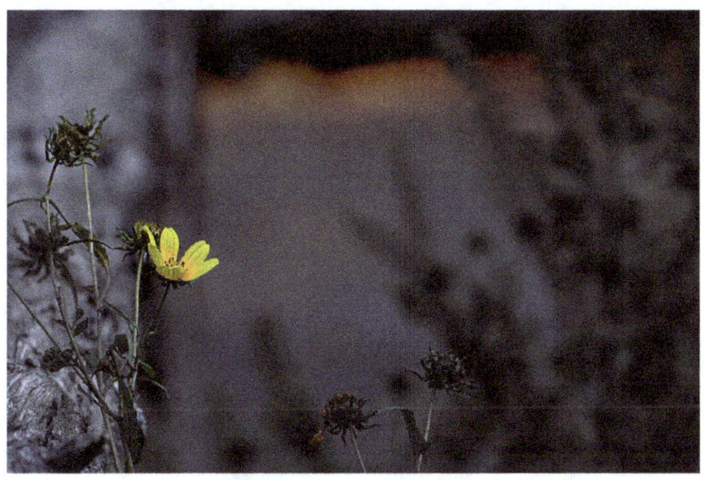

I'd hoped some couple—new in love—would come
and he, perhaps in trying to coerce
affection, would recite some lavish verse
and clench me with his fingertip and thumb
and pinch my stem and place me in her hair
or hold me to her nose as if my scent
would somehow lure her toward his veiled intent
and I would be kept in between their stare
and be the witness to their first shy kiss
then be forever pressed inside some book
where—old in love—their clouded eyes would look
and they, in finding me, would reminisce.

No couple ever came. No kiss. No love.
Dreams like mine are what the soil is made of.

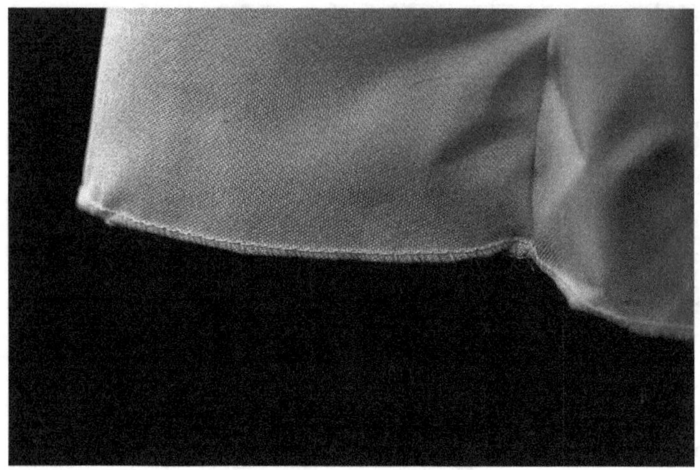

Pray—rely—as if you were
that woman twelve years ill
who, even so, had faith—was sure—
as she was bleeding, still,
that *if she could but touch His thread*
she would be made well.
He healed the sick and raised the dead—
what of a cancer cell!
Trust—believe with all your soul.
Thy faith hath made thee whole.

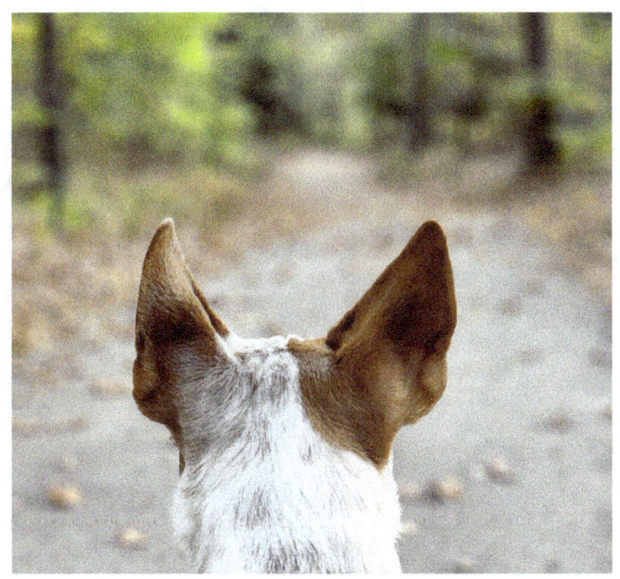

Let's go! Let's go! Come on, you say.
I let you think *you* lead the way—
turning where you say to turn
and taking treats as if to learn
things you didn't know I knew
(I act confused to humor you).
But someday you will come to see
the alpha on these walks is me.
Where I want to go, I go
(you clomp behind me yelling *no*!).
When I want to rest, I sit
(you wait, but throw your little fit).
My leash and collar have you fooled—
who's pulling and who's being pulled?

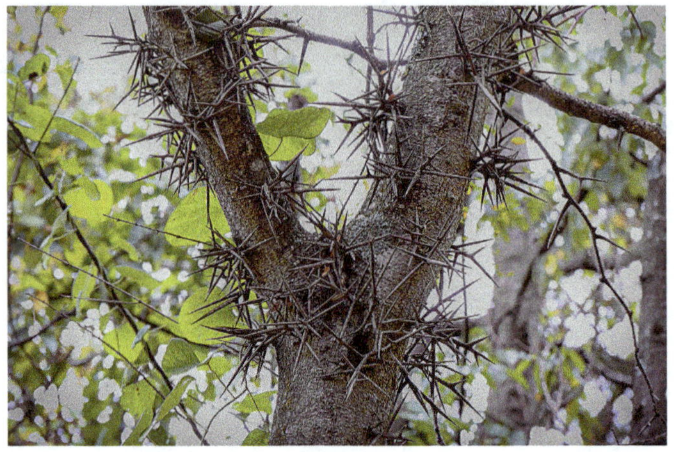

I'd like to think
you'd heard of how
they (with a wink)
had crowned His brow
with thorns that ripped
into His skin,
of how they'd whipped
and taunted Him
before they'd nailed
Him up to die—
to think you're scaled
with spikes to try
in your own way
to show Him thanks.
I know that they
(your pointed shanks)
aren't penitence—
just self-defense.

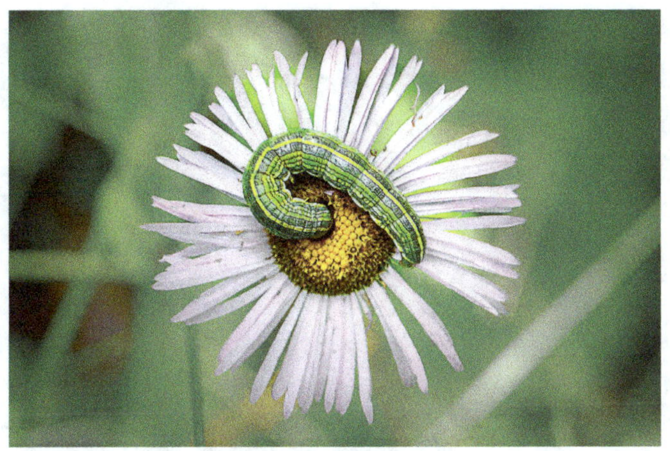

Ever since I left my shell
I've watched my body stretch and swell
(I say as if you couldn't tell)
so much so that I've split my skin.
Just when I'm through, I eat again.
In fact, this flower I'm lying in
can't bear my weight and will begin
to wilt if I don't move along.
Do you think there's something wrong?
I have this sense—inherent, strong—
I'm incomplete or don't belong
inside this self. Does that seem strange?

I have this urge to rearrange—
I have a hunch it's time for change.

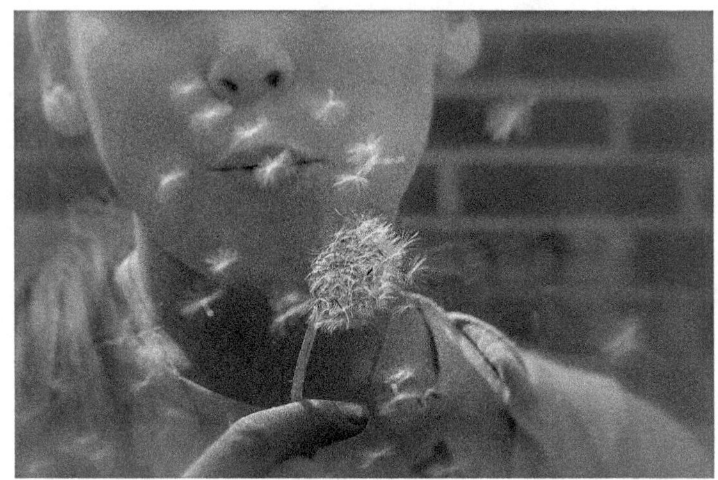

You took a tiny
breath and blew.
Away a hundred
wishes flew.
I wish that I could
turn them true—
but that is up to
God and you.

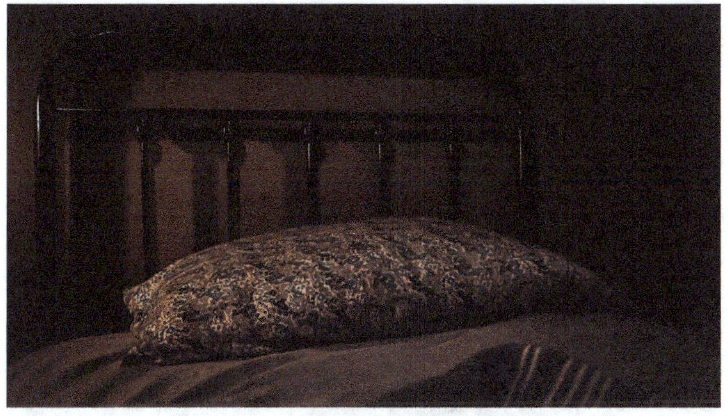

I saw you last night. You were here!

A crowd of people. None I knew.

A lot of talking. Nothing clear.

A room of strangers. Me and you.

We did not speak. We did not touch.

I am not sure you saw me there.

No hug. No sobbing tears or such.

You did not sense my speechless stare.

And then I woke. And you were gone.

How many years? Yet there you were!

I tried to hold you through a yawn.

I lost you in a drowsy blur.

How sweet. How sad. That dream-borne ache.

To almost have again. To wake.

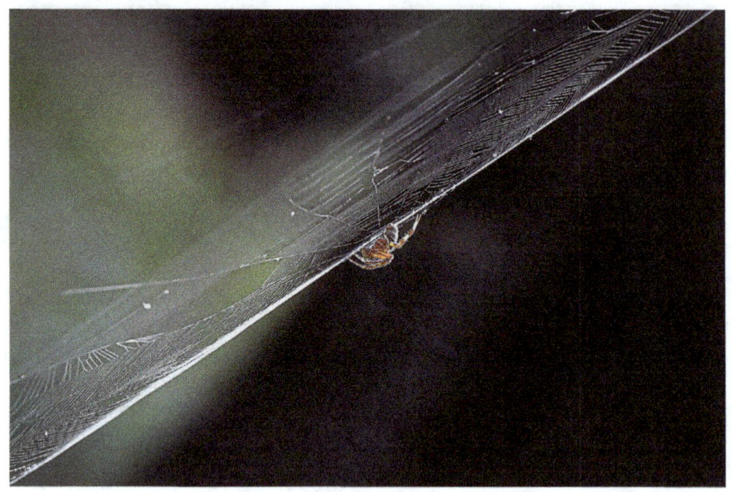

Life has taught me
of regret
enough to know
you have to let
Time and Fate
—that sly duet—
have their say
in what you get
or you are apt
to quit then fret
for what you hadn't
gotten yet.

Persistence will reward beget.
I'm not taking down this net.

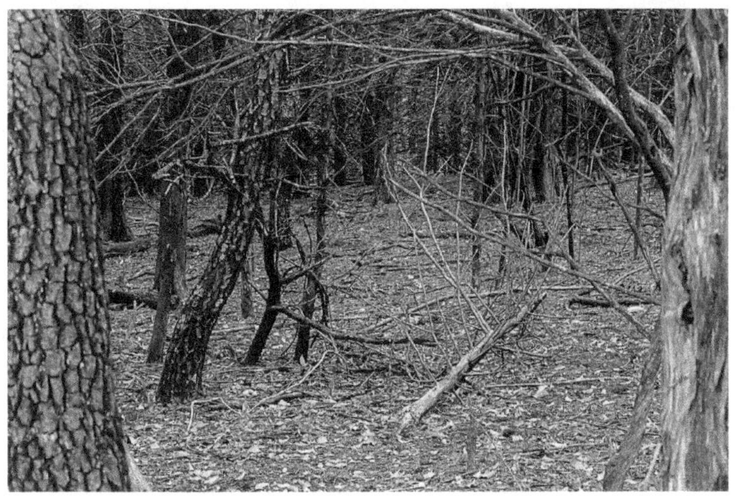

My foot step must have startled you.
Your hoof step startled me.
Our eyes locked for a breath or two,
your head cocked quizzically.
I moved to raise my camera—slow.
You must have thought *a threat.*
My picture caught the woods, but no
hint that we had met.

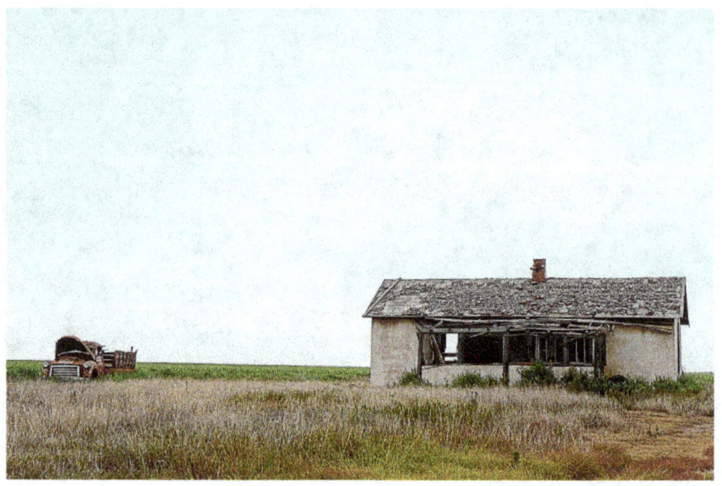

That day she left, she called me this old shack!

And then she came out here and took a whack
at *my* front windshield! Look here, here's the crack!
Do you think she killed that maniac?

I know she did! I watched her take a pack
of some white powder from a paper sack
and put it in his drink. One gulp. One hack.
She told them that he'd had a heart attack.

The way she revved that beat up Pontiac.
The way those tail lights trailed into the black.
I knew that she was never coming back.

I wonder what she ever saw in Jack?

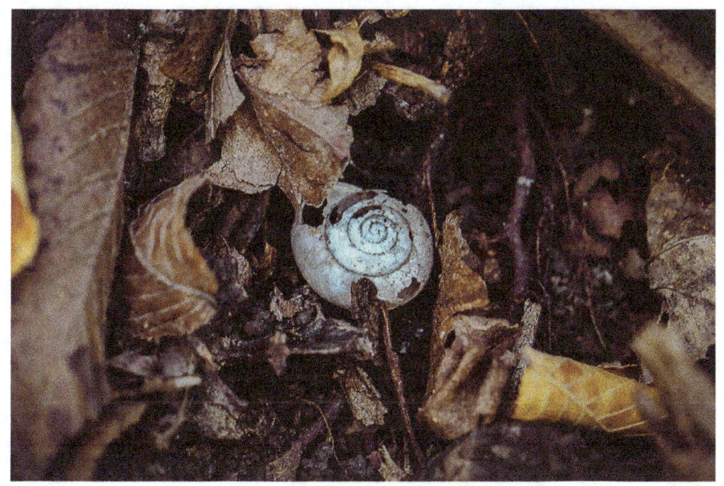

Here my emptied remnant lies
like the closet full of clothes
left when someone's someone dies
in the room where no one goes,
kept as if to fossilize
their dead inside some sealed repose
and then one day to realize
this truth that time and nature knows:
my shell will rot and fertilize—
all but the soul will decompose.

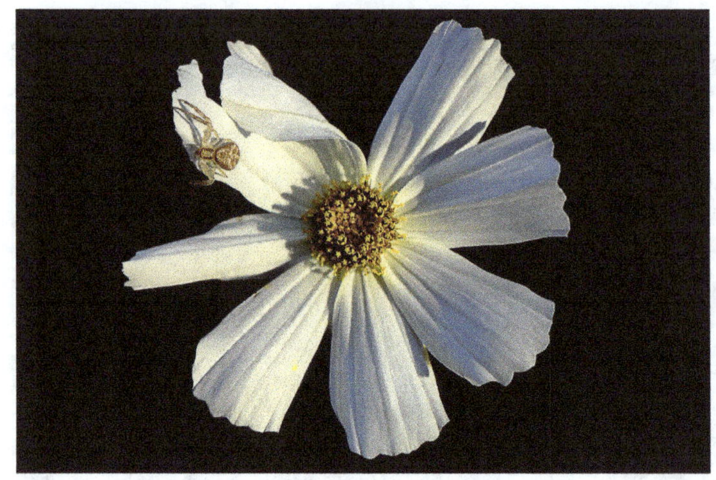

You weren't supposed to see me here.
I'm trying to blend in.
If ant or butterfly comes near
I will eat again.
I wait unwearied—white on white—
in motionless disguise
knowing something's stunned delight
will be its own demise.
Once the poor thing comes my way
I'll grab and bite it—stilled.
Oh, innocent, delicious prey—
captured . . . wounded . . . killed.

Please move along. Don't sabotage
my waxen, washed-out camouflage.

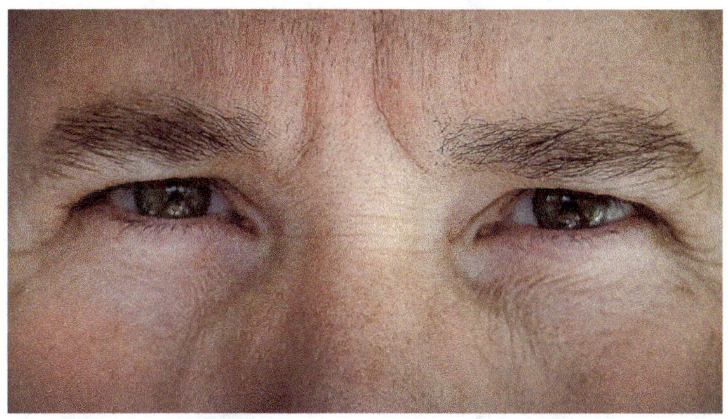

When I, from time to time, look in my eyes
I see a straining woman agonize.
Wet hair. Knees up. Her helpless husband sighs.
Through screams and tears and sweat and groans she tries.
And then a sudden stillness where she lies.
Commotion. Nurses trading soiled supplies.
And there he is! That's him I recognize.
That's *him* I see when I look in my eyes.

My father in his gown and mask disguise.
My father! And a newborn baby cries.

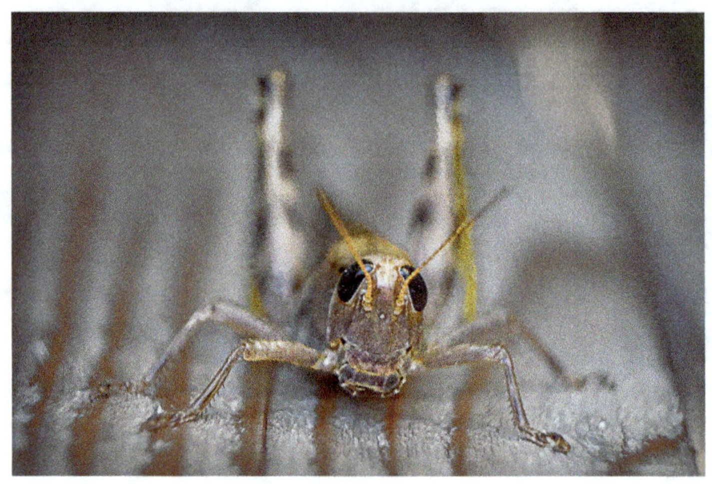

My worry is a rumbling hum
that weekly cuts the grass
with blades that threaten as they come—
killing as they pass.
Sometimes I hunker down and wait—
my chest pressed to the dirt,
praying (if it is my fate)
that dying will not hurt.
Sometimes I try my luck and jump,
not knowing where I'll fall—
hoping it is in a clump
of plants beside a wall.
There's nothing like that dreadful sound
of horror overhead!
And then it goes. I look around
to see who's maimed or dead.

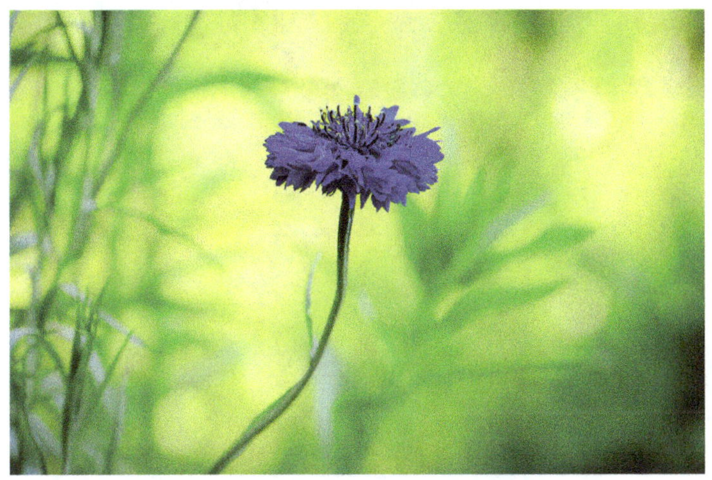

Once winter took me down I thought
I'd never live again.
My roots retained what I forgot—
the bloom that I had been.
Through months of cold and ice and snow
I languished in my doubt,
then something from above said *grow*
and I sent up a sprout.
It feels so good to stretch my stem.
The frozen dirt restricts!
Though nothing that a birded limb
and probing bee can't fix.

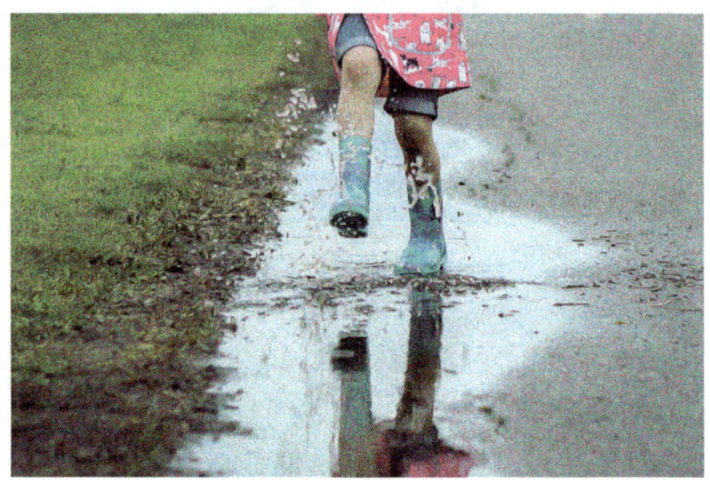

Rain will send
the rest inside
which leaves the world
to you.

Let them wonder
hollow-eyed
as you go
splashing through.

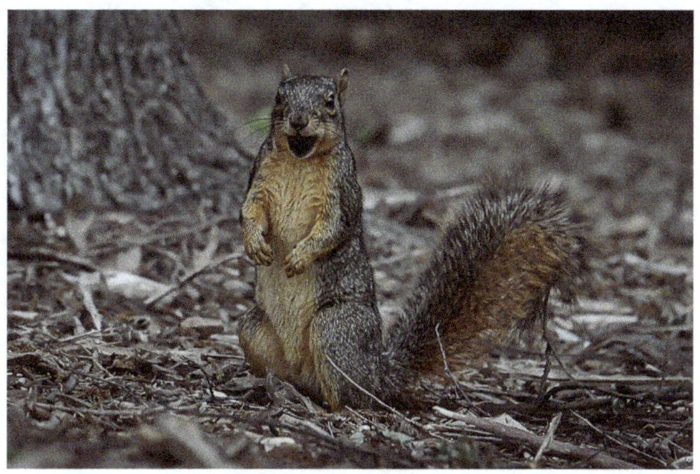

Last year they winked and told me where
to bury my supplies:
I'd put some there and put some there,
they said with scheming eyes.
And with an underhanded air
they said it would be wise
for me to store enough to share
in case the other guys
figured wrong or weren't aware
of coming snow-filled skies.
I toiled my tail off to prepare
but then to my surprise
they came and stripped my stockpiles bare!
This year when they advise

that I should work for *their* welfare
(i.e. to communize)
I'll hide my rations with great care
and dodge my own demise.

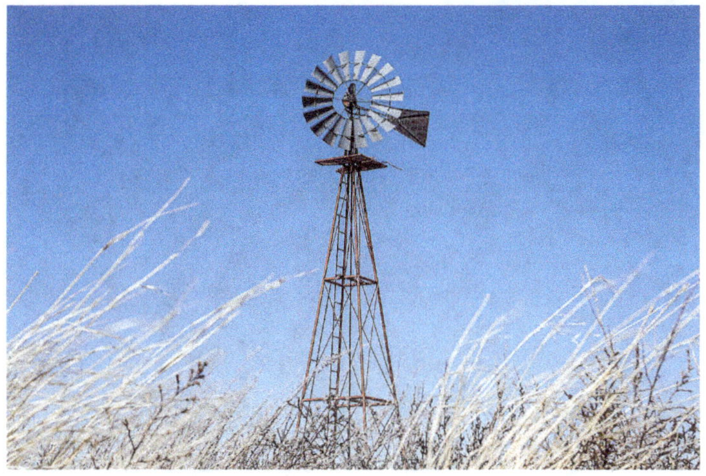

From some imbalanced highs and lows
a breeze, a gust, a wind-storm grows.
The people in its dust-filled throes
turn a hunched, contorted pose
to block the sand from eyes and nose
with stretched out fragments of their clothes
and all the while my spinning goes—
whirring as the tall grass blows
(a sound the timeworn memory knows
from standing out in shriveled rows).

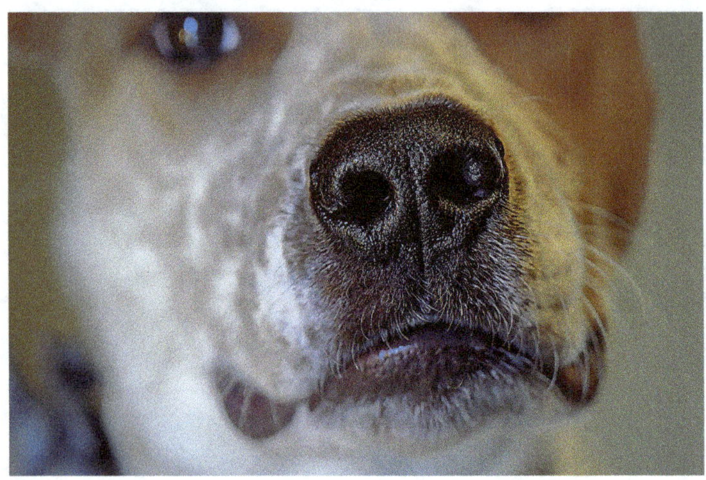

I'll give you that I'm young, but not naïve.
I saw those white hairs sticking to your sleeve
(the ones you picked at but could not unweave
when you came back from your little leave).
What tricks can she perform? Sit? Stay? Retrieve?
Lie down? Play dead? Deceive? Deceive?! Deceive?!!
You act as if I err or misperceive.

But from your first returning I could tell
(you did not wash your hands off very well).
I'd guess some trashy terrier by her smell.

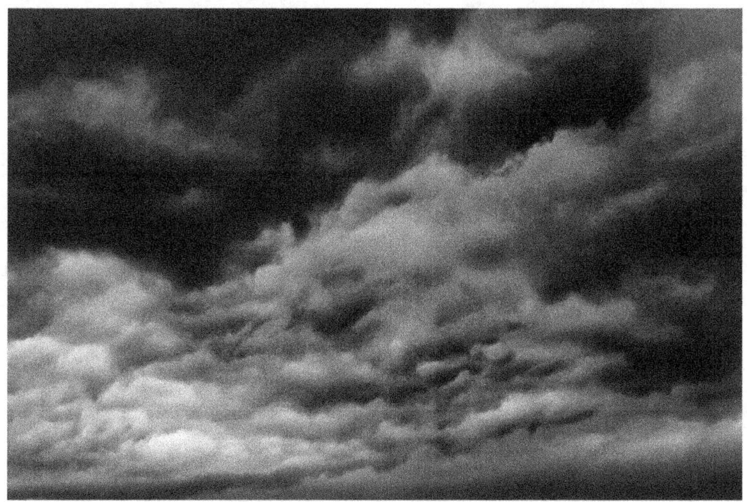

When I see clouds like this I know
rain like rocks will fiercely fall
and howling wind will wildly blow
to bang hard hail against the wall
and heap it up like frozen snow.

A distant train will darkly crawl
along its track, rumbling low.
Its echoed horn (its siren call)
at first far-off will louder grow
into a blare and scare us all.

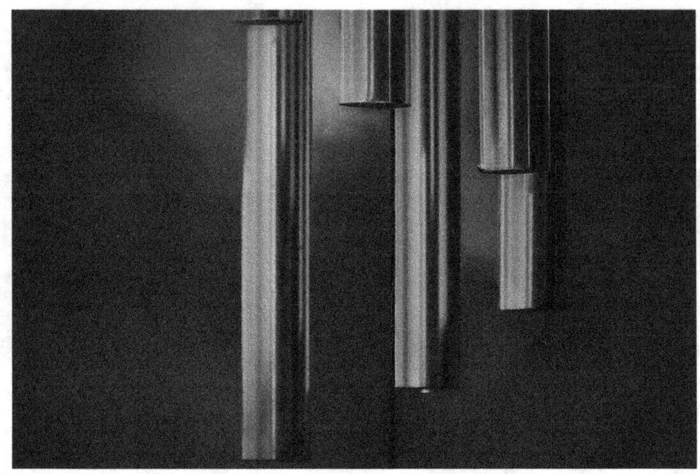

I heard you at my window screen,
whistling for me.
I heard you rustling in between
what leaves still clutch my tree.
I heard you swing my neighbor's gate
back and forth—the latch
jangling at the jarring weight
that it could not catch.
I heard you howling down the flue
like a tortured soul.
I found the damper rod and drew
it shut to seal the hole.
I heard you fighting with my chimes
late into the night,
clashing like the clanking rhymes
I was trying to write.

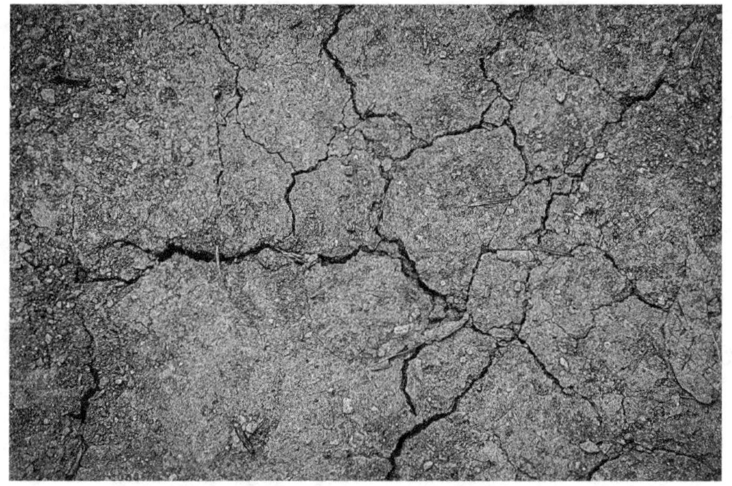

Perhaps someday a seed will drop
into one of my cracks
and rain will splatter—splash and plop—
in overflowing tracks
that turn my crust to fertile earth.
Perhaps that seed will sprout
and you will see my inner worth
slowly rising out.
Perhaps someday that seed will grow
into a lively tree
and birds will lodge there—high and low—
and everyone will see
what came of what was barren ground.
Perhaps someday. But now
I scorch and dream to hear the sound
of sparrows in that bough.

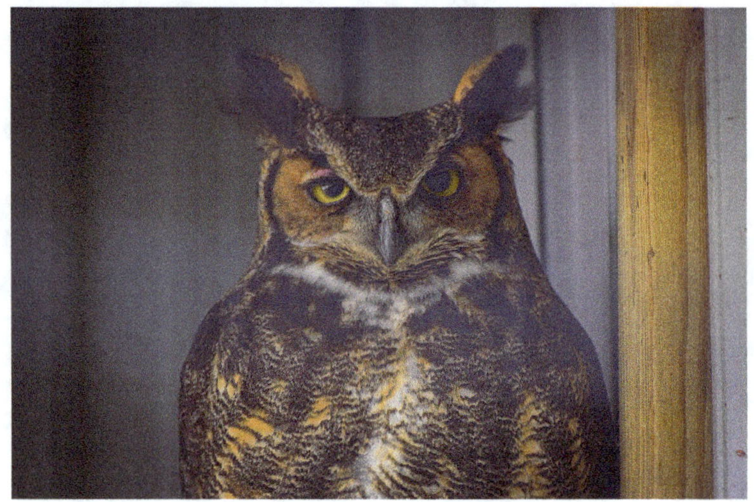

I used to hunt the whole night through.
Darkened corners squirmed and grew
as one scared mouse turned into two
and then another. They all knew
my looming presence and withdrew
in hopes of hiding from my view.
Shadows shivered when I flew.
Now I'm perched here in this zoo.
One by one I stare at you,
indifferent to your *whoo whoo whoo.*

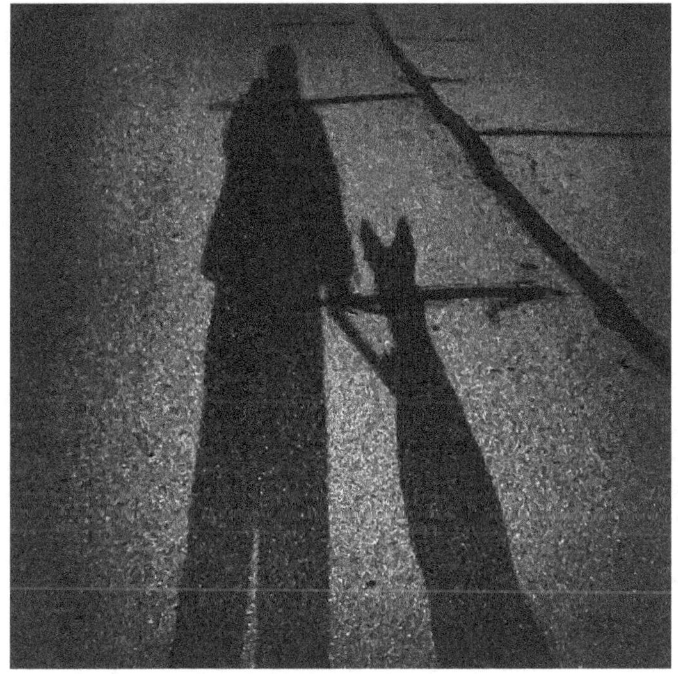

His staggered step is led by scent,
erratic like the hounds you see
running through the woods intent
on catching crook with deputy.
He must think we're on patrol,
as if the neighborhood relies
on our night and morning stroll
to be its probing ears and eyes.
He tracks down every rock and stick
and bottle cap and struggling bug
and heaves at rabbit, hop-step quick,
as I heave back against his tug.

Our shadows slant as we head back.
All is well on Quanah street.
Our house. Our porch. His leash falls slack.
He sits—*good boy*—and gets his treat.

Rain to flood along the fence.
Change to mud the fissured dirt.
Drop buckets for each day of drought.
Lightning that was hidden since
last spring—strike down! Disconcert
the frightened faces peering out.
Spill the gutters. Overflow
the creek banks. Pound the roof.
Swamp the grass and soak the crops.
Pour enough for us to know
our prayers were answered—drench us proof!
Ignore us when we pray it stops.

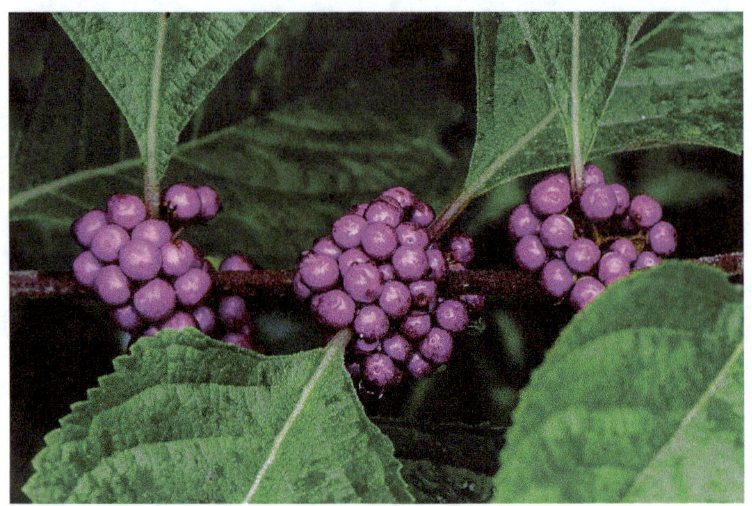

Save us now, if you are Christ!

For us, this is a fitting price.
But look—he is a sacrifice.
Consider me—remember, Lord—
when you reach your right reward.

This day we'll meet in paradise.

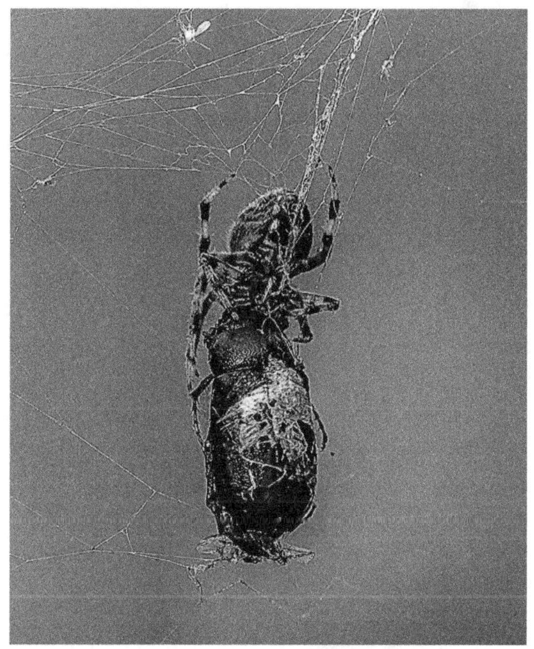

I've felt the snag of web across my face.
I've plucked and pulled at strings that seemed to go
from ear to ear like some wig weaved of lace—
the more I picked, the more it seemed to grow.
I've dealt with one eye weeping like Frost wrote
when strands have crossed me as I walked a wood.
What words I've said those times one should not quote
(they're vile and—in that state—not understood!).
And yet I've never failed to wriggle free
from any spider's web I've come across.

Dreams Like Mine

I've never had a spider capture me.
Stupefy me. Then shroud me—limp—in floss.
So why—in seeing you caught in this thread—
did it feel so much like I was dead?

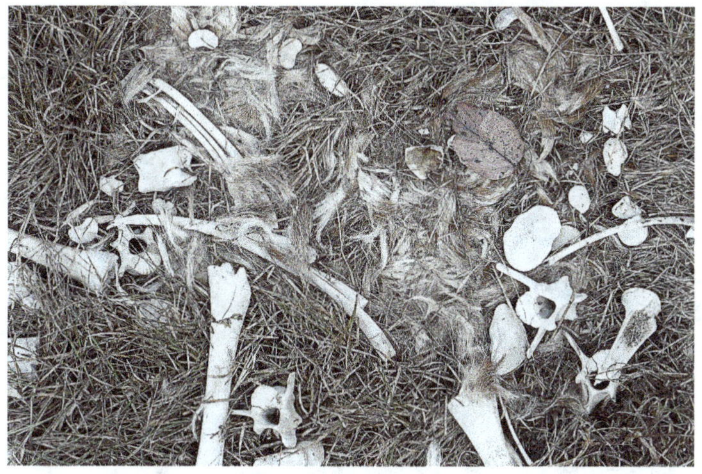

Twigs and dry leaves crackled to the stir
of skittish squirrels hiding in the trees.
Clustered bagworms clothed a conifer,
gaunt like an old man beaten by disease.
One butterfly—heartbreaking voyageur—
sought missing flowers, tossed by unseen seas.
From somewhere faint, a bird song would recur
as if to put an anxious soul at ease.
I walked into the field and there you were—
the startle of you made my footsteps freeze.
You were but a batch of bones and fur—
your meat picked clean, some hunger to appease.

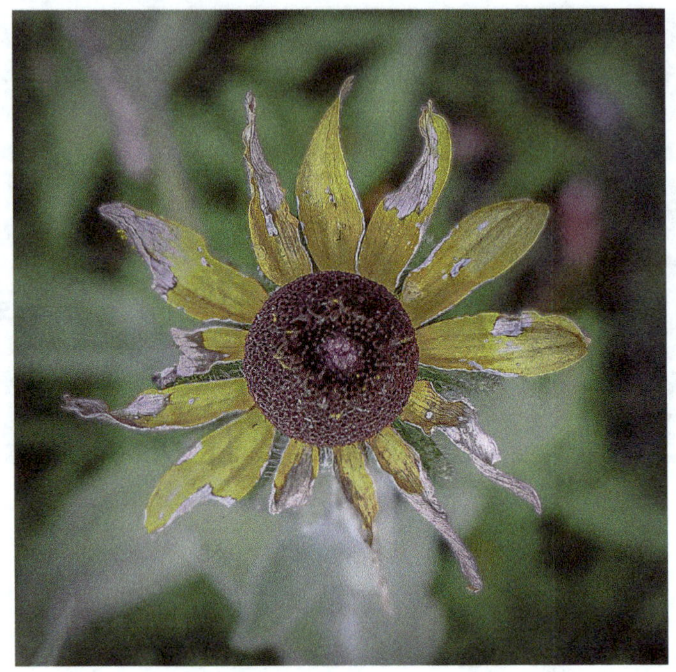

My younger days I now lament.
I wither with my petals bent
and dry and void of any scent
and nearly all my color spent.
The bee still comes in brief descent,
perhaps by love or accident,
but leaves in hurried discontent.

I wilt and wonder where time went.

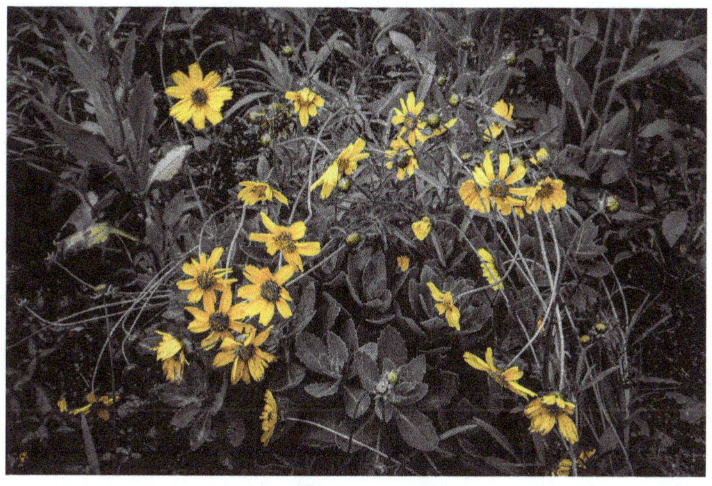

The first drops came—what did we know?
We liked the sound and liked the smell.
We'd heard that rain would help us grow
(having bloomed a week or so,
we did not grasp the weather well—
so recent in the soil below).
The droplets glanced us soft and slow
like dripping pearls in parallel.
Then the wind began to blow.
Tree limbs twisted to and fro!
Leaves then twigs then branches fell!
We slumped and put our heads down low,
praying for the storm to go.
We watched the water pool and swell
and felt the mud beneath us flow
(our roots opposed the undertow).

And then it eased enough to tell
that we would have some scars to show
and we were bent—but standing though.

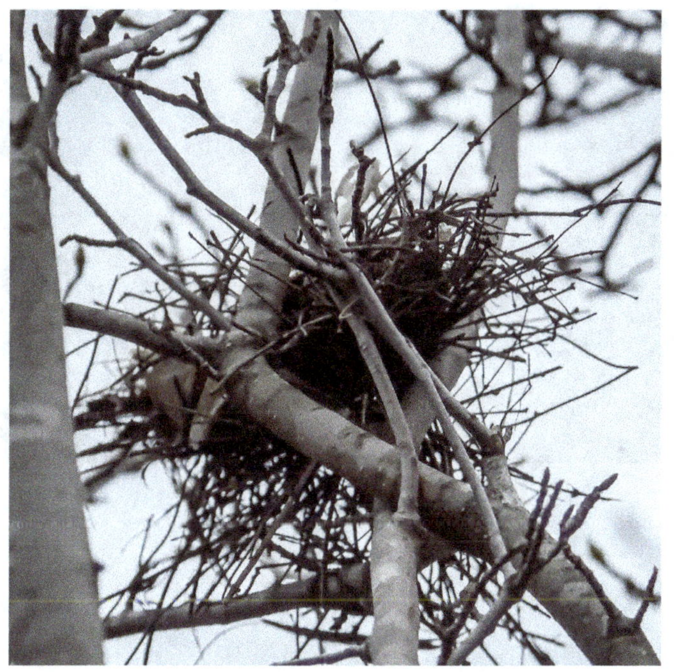

When I started stacking sticks, I knew.
When I saw each tiny beak break through.
When your first few fledgling feathers grew.
I knew.
I knew. I knew. I knew. I knew!
Then I counted four. Then three. Then two.
Then one. Then nature gave her callous cue
(and somehow hurt me, even though *I knew*!).
My little one—the last—flapped wings
and flew.

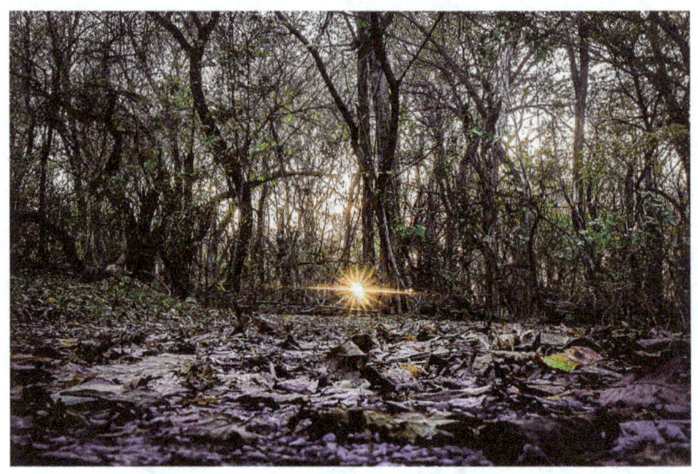

This year's leaves are underfoot,
trampled black by soggy boot
and shoe that slogged through last week's rain,
once green and new—now but a stain
to integrate into the ground.

The trees stand still and make no sound.

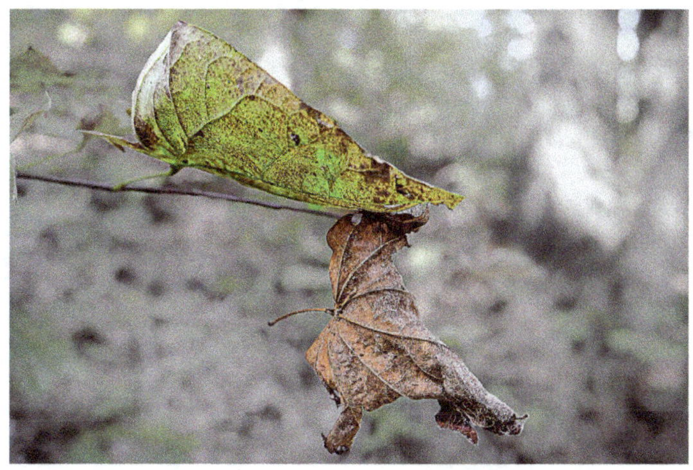

I knew my green would fade and I
would wither—curled and brown and dry—
as summer days drew further on.
I knew the stem through which I'd drawn
my water would one day be barred
of any flow. I'd seen the yard
littered with the leaves that went
before me in their whirled descent.
I knew some gust would one day blow
and I would give my grip and go.

I knew that fate would soon detach me—
I did not know that you would catch me.

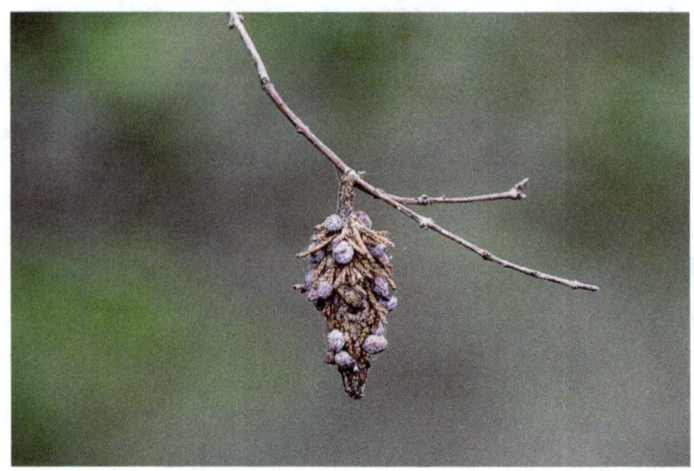

I spent last April fabricating
my cocoon—and decorating
so that it was integrating
with the tree where I was waiting
for the week I'd spend pupating
(veiled by leaf and berry plating).

Then would come my liberating—
my search to find a worm worth mating.
Then eggs. And then our separating
followed by our terminating.

And all the while obliterating
this poor tree I'm infiltrating.

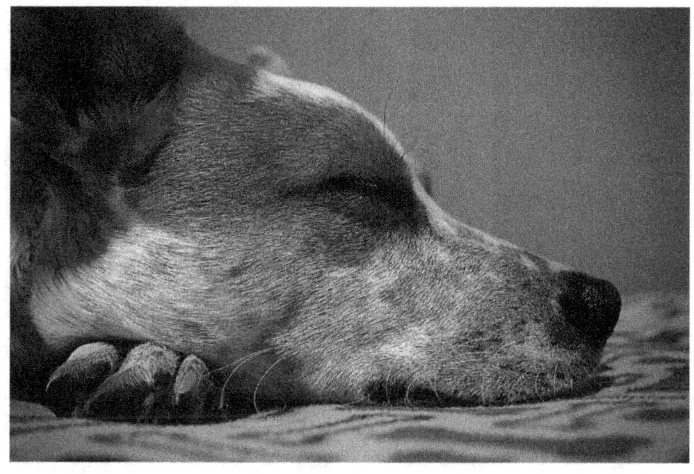

When my eyelid starts to twitch
I'm watching you. You're choosing which
coat to wear.
When I raise and turn my ear
I fear I heard you disappear
on the stair.
When I whimper whining yaps
You're back! I hear clinked keys! Perhaps
the dog walk pair.
When my paws flinch back and pump
I'm running to you and I jump
on your chair.
When I woof and wag my tail
I see our park. Our woods. Our trail.
We are there!

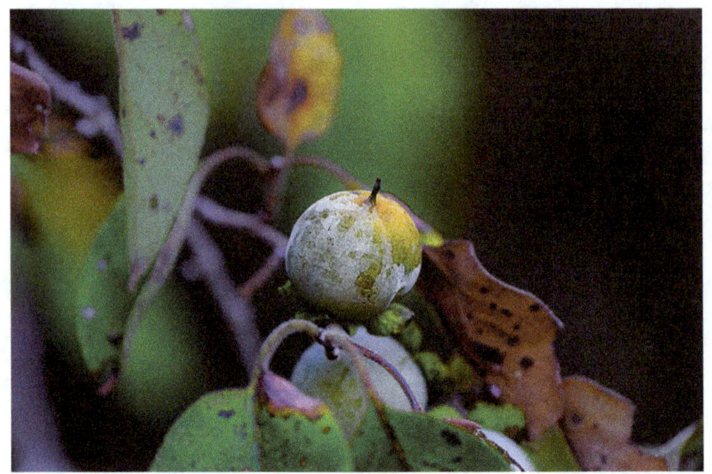

Strip the trees of rusted leaves.
Take the shriveled petals down.
Bead the web the spider weaves
with mist that hides our little town.
Chill the morning air so breath
hangs heavy like a lowly cloud.
Let one cricket sing of death
from a field once millions loud.
Set the V-shaped geese in flight.
Scatter squirrels to hide their stores.
Bring Orion to his height
and streak the sky with meteors.
Give my trees a windblown shake.
Get me busy with my rake.

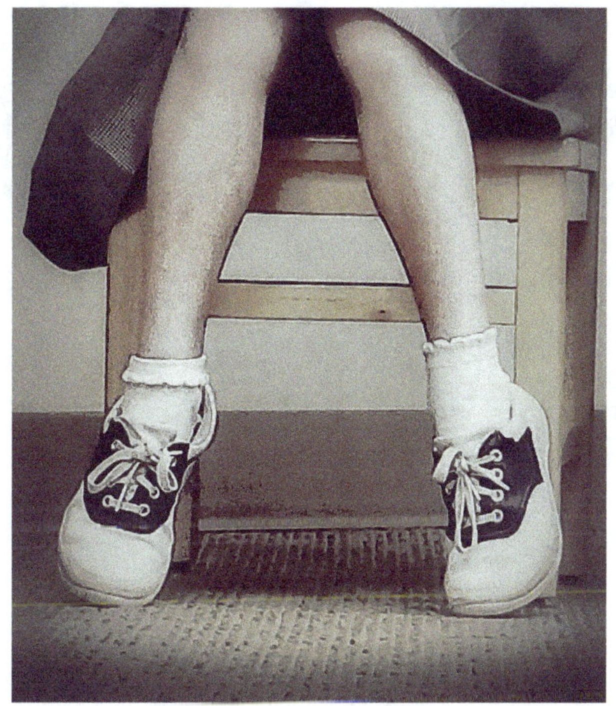

Little smile. Little nose.
Little feet on tippy toes.
Little pencil mark that shows
how tall she is—how short time grows.
Little left, my reason knows,
before some little car horn blows.
Little wave and off she goes.

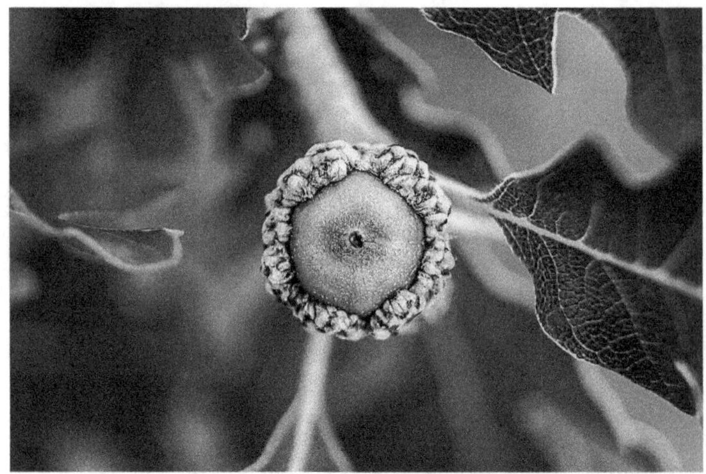

Come wild wind and pry around
enough to toss me to the ground.
Come stashing squirrel or jay and set
me in loose soil and then forget
the way to where you've hidden me.
Come sun. Come rain. Set my root free
and let my leafy shoot grow tall.
Come God to guide it all.
Come curious child to say *Wait--but*
how'd that tree come from a nut?

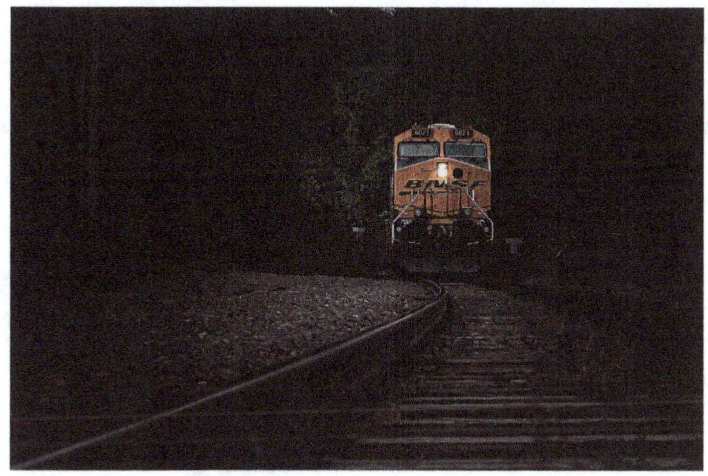

Along the riverbank it
snakes.
The bend and then the bridge it
makes.
A dog beside the shanty
wakes.
Closer—but how long it
takes.
And then the light! The ballast
quakes.
And louder screech the wheels and
brakes.
Beside the track my footing
shakes.
And then it goes. Oh, my heart
aches.

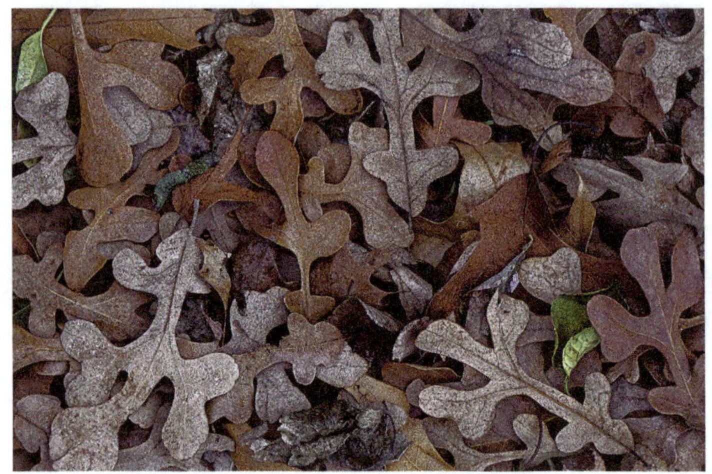

I found a thousand fallen leaves
piled beneath a tree.
I saw above me branches where
they were supposed to be.
Two or three were lost to wind
despite my fumbling chase,
the rest—although I strained to reach—
I could not put in place.
In time I crumpled with the leaves
(they were downed by weather),
yielding to this truth: some things
cannot go back together.

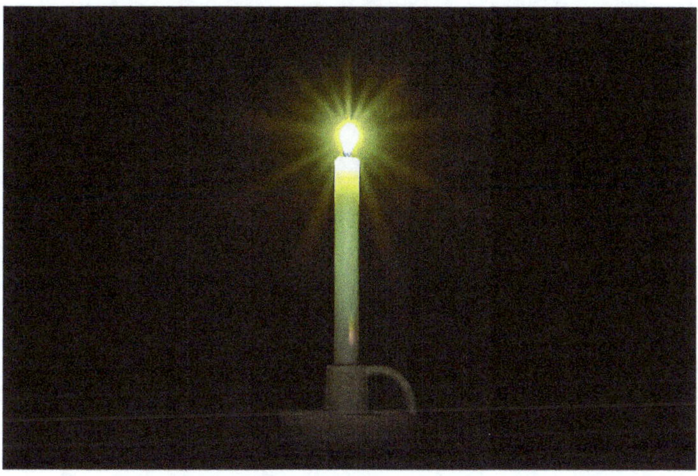

Light flickers on the window glass and walls.
I sit beside the candle in its glow
and watch the flame as it coils up and falls.
Without you here, days drag. The hours are slow.

The room is small and quiet in the spark
of one slight flame atop a candlestick.
The world is cold and empty in the dark
beyond the reaches of the burning wick.

I check the clock and see the time is late.
I set the lock and draw the window shade.
The dog turns twice and settles in his crate.
I face another night. Alone. Afraid.

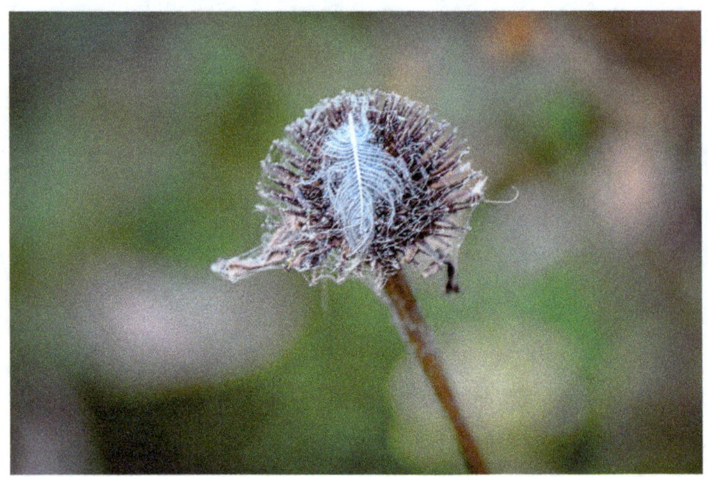

I bet you'd thought you'd caught a snowflake.
No—not in this warm weather.
Some bird in flight or rousing shake
must have lost its feather.

With November will come cold.
Perchance some clouded day
a real snowflake—air tossed and rolled—
by fate will float your way.

Then you can see how different
the flake and feather felt—
and how, by wind, the feather went
and how the flake, by melt.

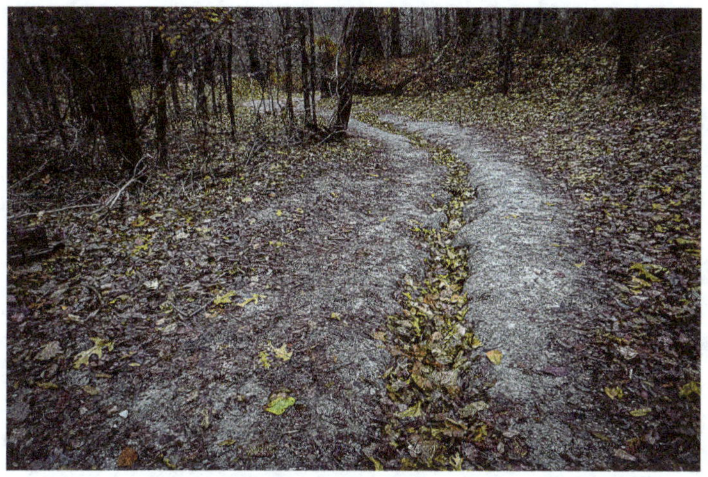

The chiseled rivulet which formed
downhill on the trail from rain
that burst from buckets when it stormed
last spring was running once again
when I walked the path today.
Well, say at least the trench was filled
with leaves that seemed as if to play
like they were currents sloshed and spilled
against the banks as they gushed forth
(the stream was an illusion, though,
crafted by the wind from north
that blew them in their southward flow).
My inner child said play along
and no one was around to see:
I kicked against the gushes—strong—
as if the leaves were soaking me.

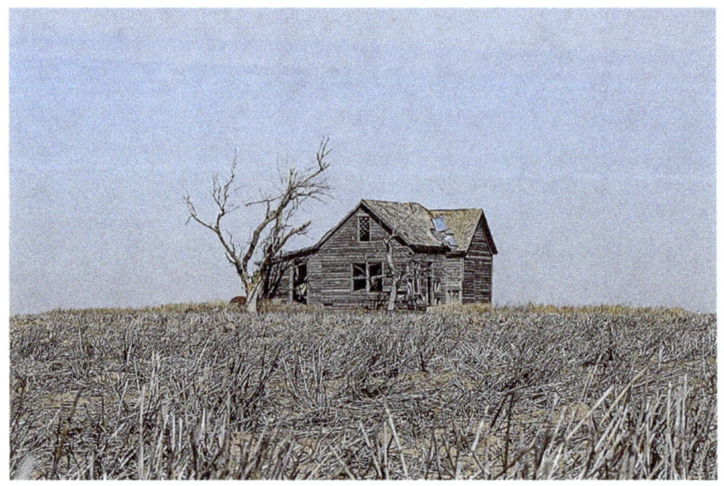

I sometimes wish a cigarette
tossed from some passing car would set
the fields on fire and winds would turn
the flames to me and I would burn.
Or that the clouds would billow tall
and from them let a funnel fall
to work the dirt and wipe it clean
and wreck me like I'd never been.
Oh, if the kids would slam my door
and stomp their feet across my floor
and run amuck and scream and yell!
This growing old—this life—is hell.
It is too quiet with you gone.
The days go on and on and on.
I breathe a dusty, gasping hiss
and creak and groan and reminisce.

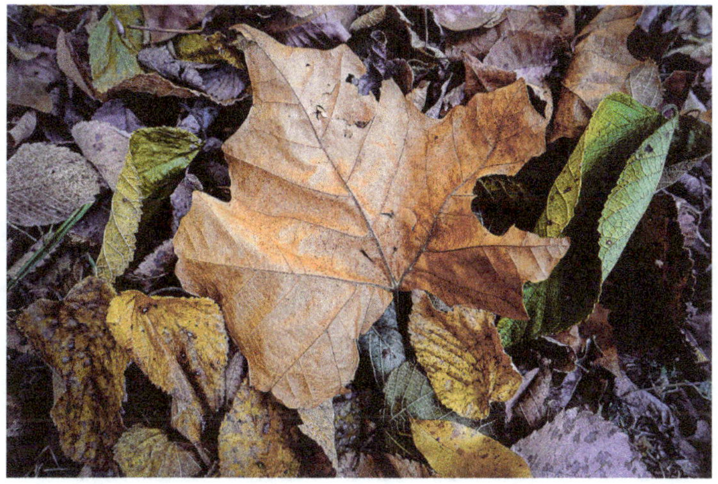

Were
I six
and finding you
I'd get sticks and poke them through,
making sails to move my boat
over whales
that sink
and float
in oceans
made
by hose and hole. I'm afraid the honest toll
of life, of age, of time, of years (when wonder turns to disbelief)
is that our child-self disappears and then a leaf
is just a leaf.

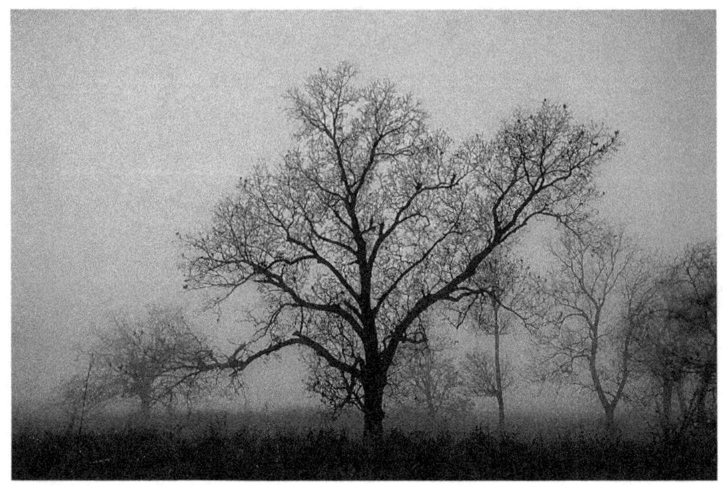

I wish you'd seen me back in spring
or summer—when my branches bent
beneath a bulk of baggy leaves.
My trunk swayed in wind-swept heaves
and from my crowded crown there went
the steady sigh of me breathing.

Fall has stripped me thin and bare
save some few leaves (my souvenirs)
I hold but am resigned to drop.
Gone are my looks. My shaggy top.
Wind blows through but no one hears.
I sense your awkward, vacant stare.

I wish you'd seen me months ago—
or perhaps disguised in snow.

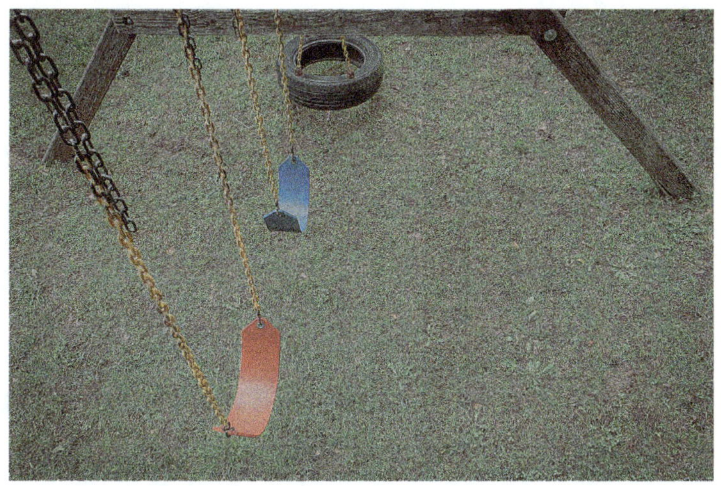

I'm guessing you will be in class that day
or in some coffee shop out with your friends.
It will be several years you've been away.
I'll call some guy a neighbor recommends
who does this sort of thing—takes childhood down
and stacks it in the back of some old truck
and hauls it to some dump outside of town.
I will crowd the kitchen window, struck
by the empty footprint in the grass.
And I'll imagine seeing little you
smiling, laughing with each swinging pass.
I will stare and know those days are through.

I'll tell you—as if nothing—on some call
while sitting on the floor against the wall.

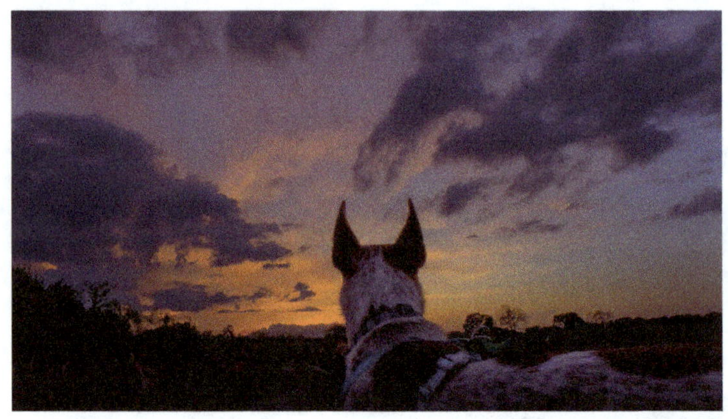

You pulled me past the cottontail
that cut across our wooded trail
and sprang into the undergrowth—
so close it nearly tripped us both!
You yanked my leash which made me drop
the stick I'd snatched and would not stop
to let me snatch it up again.
No time to sniff a snake's shed skin.
You chided me for any try
to scratch or bite my itching thigh—
prodding with your poking hand.
But when we came to open land
You stopped. You let my leash fall slack.
You laid your arm across my back.
No noise—save some dog's distant bark.
We sat to watch the day go dark.

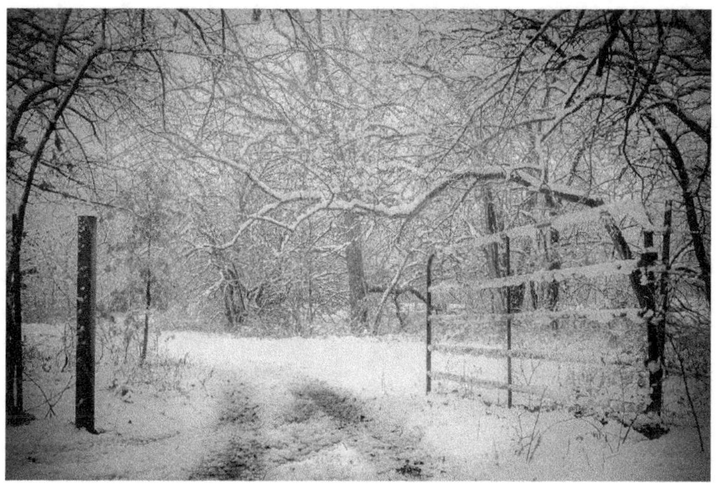

There's something sad
about a track
of tires through
a fall of snow.

The thought of pausing.
Looking back.
Then driving on
and letting go.

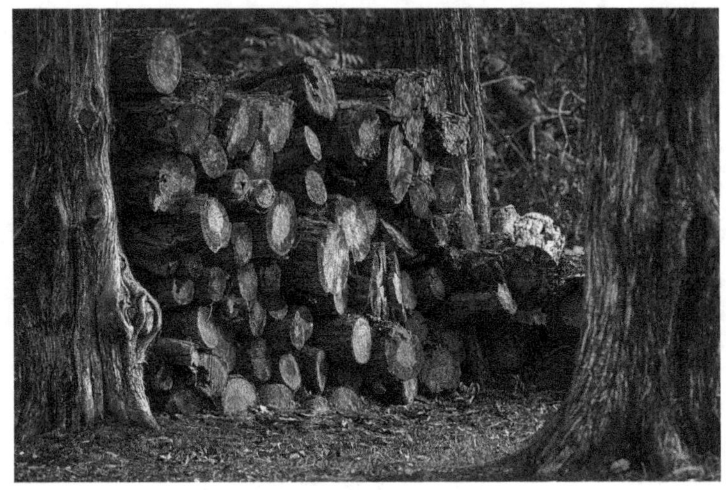

Stack me in your firebox
on crumpled paper shreds.
Double up your thickest socks.
Hat your gray haired heads.
Strike a match and hold it low.
Set the shreds on fire.
Poke me with a rod and blow.
Make the flames grow higher.
Draw the shade and watch the white
gather at the glass.
Sit together. Pass the night
watching snow amass.

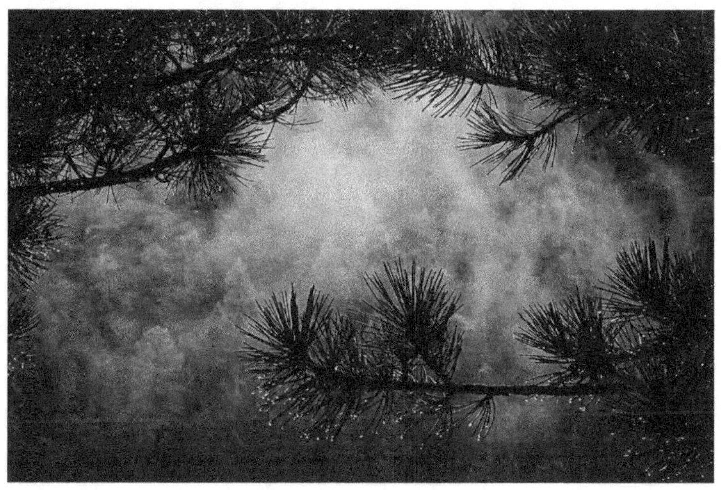

Life is but a fog, a mist
that early of a morning lies
so thick, so dense one would insist
it has no end. The old, the wise
know that by noon the vapors spread—
the sun burns through and hazes lift.
Like that—a day, a life, has fled.
Vanished—gone—this fleeting gift.

Life is but a mist, a breath
that dwindles between birth and death.

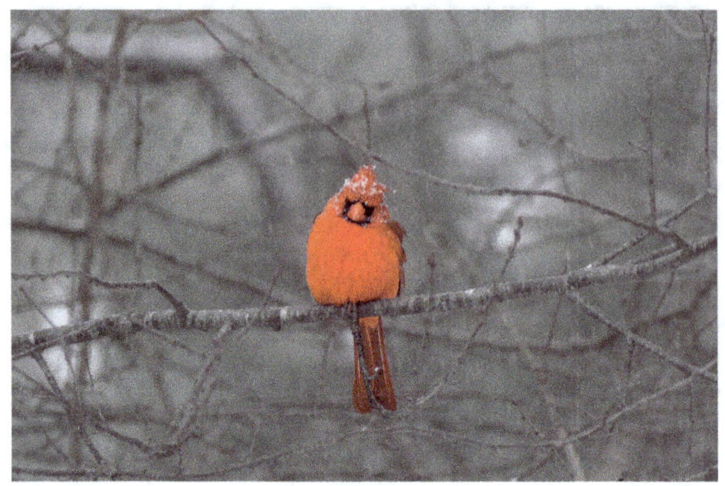

Something in your
silent flight—
the way you took
your leafless height
above the frigid,
frozen blight
and flicked your crest
to fling off white
told me you would
be all right.

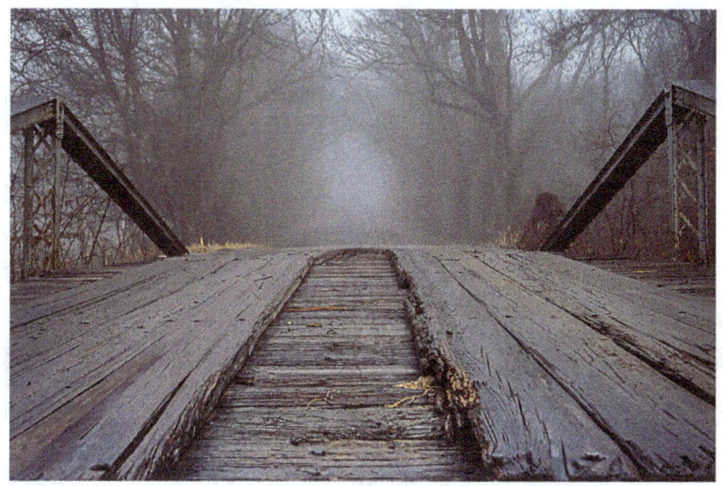

Behind you fades
the former year.
Your future
lies ahead.
Beyond this bridge
may not be clear.
What to
do instead?
Love the ones
you still have here.
Venerate
your dead.
Face what's coming.
Persevere.
Oh, and
make your bed.

We knew from daybreak that your light was lent.
We played like children—guileless, innocent—
as you made your gradual ascent
and reached your peak. Then the slow torment
of watching and lamenting your descent—
of wanting back the minutes we misspent
or wasted without purpose or intent.
As if not knowing what our praying meant,
you dropped behind the trees—and paused—then went.

www.ingramcontent.com/pod-product-compliance
Lightning Source LLC
LaVergne TN
LVHW050542100826
845148LV00002B/648

* 9 7 9 8 3 8 5 2 5 5 8 1 8 *